CONTENTS

UNDER THE SEA

Brian Williams

Published 1979 by Warwick Press, 730 Fifth Avenue,
New York 10019
First published in Great Britain by Ward Lock in 1978
Copyright © 1978 by Grisewood & Dempsey Ltd
Printed in Italy by New Interlitho, Milan
6 5 4 3 2 1 All rights reserved

WARWICK PRESS · NEW YORK

8/79

Library of Congress Catalog Card No. 78–67839
ISBN 0–531–09133–3
ISBN 0–531–09118–X lib. bdg.

Graham Allen

Exploring the Depths

The ocean covers almost three-quarters of the Earth. Yet we are only just beginning to explore the undersea world.

On the ocean floor are wide plains, deep valleys and high mountains. In most places the sea is so deep that the weight of water above would crush an ordinary submarine. Only special diving craft called bathyscaphes can explore the ocean depths.

The bathyscaphe *Trieste* has dived to over 35,000 feet in the Mariana Trench in the Pacific Ocean. (The sea here would easily cover the top of Mount Everest, which rises to a height of 29,028 feet.)

Trieste is controlled rather like an underwater balloon. It has a small cabin fixed beneath a large tank full of gasoline (which is lighter than water). It carries steel pellets as ballast (weight), and dives by flooding its ballast tanks with water. To surface, pellets are released. The craft becomes lighter and, just as a gas-filled balloon rises, the gasoline "float" carries *Trieste* upwards.

It is so dark on the ocean floor that many deep-sea fish have no need of sight. The bathyscaphe has powerful lights to probe the inky darkness.

The shallow continental shelf lies closest to land. Beyond it, the ocean floor slopes down steeply to the deep sea plains. The sea-bed, like the land, has plains, mountains, volcanoes, chasms and trenches. The deepest part is called the abyss.

The Continental Shelf

Around the great land masses called continents lies an area of land that is covered by shallow seas. This is the continental shelf. The sea here is only about 590 feet deep. Beyond the edge of the shelf, the ocean floor slopes away into much deeper water. In places the shelf stretches over 600 miles from the shore.

More undersea plants and animals live on the continental shelf than in any other part of the ocean. The water is fairly warm and sunlit, and there is plenty of food. Some food i washed into the sea by rivers which pour mud and sand on to the shelf

Tiny animals and plants called plankton drift near the surface There are fish and other swimming animals such as seals, whales and squid. These swimming creature are called nekton. On the sea-bed live sponges, starfish, crabs, lobsters, limpets, worms and many other creatures. They are known a benthos, and they feed on small par

sponge

edible crab

sea urchin

lobster

starfish

praw

common octopus

6

Portuguese man-of-war

cles of food that drift down from bove. Some move about the ocean oor. Others cling to rocks or burow into the mud.

The octopus and starfish try to tch shellfish with their long ucker-studded tentacles. But wary callops may escape by snapping ut their shells and shooting out a t of water to propel them out of each. The Portuguese man-of-war a dangerous kind of jellyfish hich paralyzes its prey with its inging tentacles.

scallop

flounder

sea
anemone

cod

brittle-star

sea squirt

The Darkest Deep

In the ocean deeps, below about 5000 feet, it is cold and dark. There is no sunlight, so there are no plants. (Plants need sunlight to make their food.) In this gloomy world live strange fishes.

Food is scarce, and the fishes live by scavenging (eating dead creatures) or by preying on smaller fishes. Many have gaping jaws and can stretch their stomachs to swallow prey much bigger than themselves. Some are cannibals that eat their own kind.

Most deep-sea fishes are small. To attract prey, some use luminous lures. Others are blind and find food by waving their long feelers.

All the deep-sea creatures in the picture have glowing lights on their bodies. Scientists call this "bioluminescence" or "living light".

A Coral Reef

Beneath the clear waters of the warm tropical seas lies the strange and beautiful world of the coral reef. Coral looks like rock. But it is actually made from the skeletons of tiny sea animals called polyps.

The coral polyp is related to the sea anemone. It begins life as a floating larva. Later it sinks to the sea-bed and clings to a rock. It covers its soft body with an "outside skeleton" of hard limestone.

The polyp's stinging tentacles look like the petals of a flower. With its tentacles, the polyp catches even smaller sea creatures and pushes them into its mouth. Each polyp makes "buds" from which new polyps grow.

When a polyp dies, its hard skeleton remains. Over many years millions of skeletons pile up into an ever-growing wall or "reef". Reefs close to shore are called fringe reefs. Farther out to sea, great barrier reefs form. The largest reef in the world is the Great Barrier Reef of Australia. Reefs shaped like rings or horseshoes are called atolls. Sometimes the coral forms an island.

Corals grow in many shapes and colors. Together they look like an underwater "forest". Many plants, fish and other sea creatures find food and shelter on the reefs. But their home is sometimes threatened by the chief enemy of the coral, the crown-of-thorns starfish. This creature eats the polyps and causes the reef first to die and then to crumble slowly under the force of the waves.

gaterins

blue-ringed octopus

surgeon fish

zebra fish

lion fish

giant clam

seahorses

spiny sea
urchin

feather
stars

crown-of-thorns
starfish

13

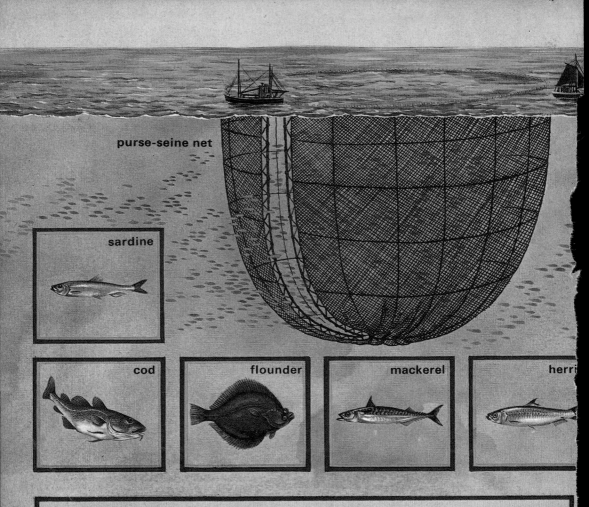

purse-seine net

sardine

cod

flounder

mackerel

herri[ng]

The Ocean's Store

There is more than enough food in the sea to feed all the Earth's people. But so far we have not made full use of the ocean's store.

For thousands of years fishermen have caught fish in nets. Today they use three main types of net: the purse-seine (which is pulled around the fish and closed like a string bag), the trawl (which is dragged along underwater), and the gill or drift net (which hangs down in the sea like a curtain). Near the shore, fish are also caught on long lines of hooks.

Some of the most important food fish are shown here. Modern fishing boats use radar and sonar (sound waves) to find where the shoals are. So many fish are being caught that some kinds have become scarce.

A better way to harvest food from the sea is to have underwater "farms" where fish are bred and reared in cages.

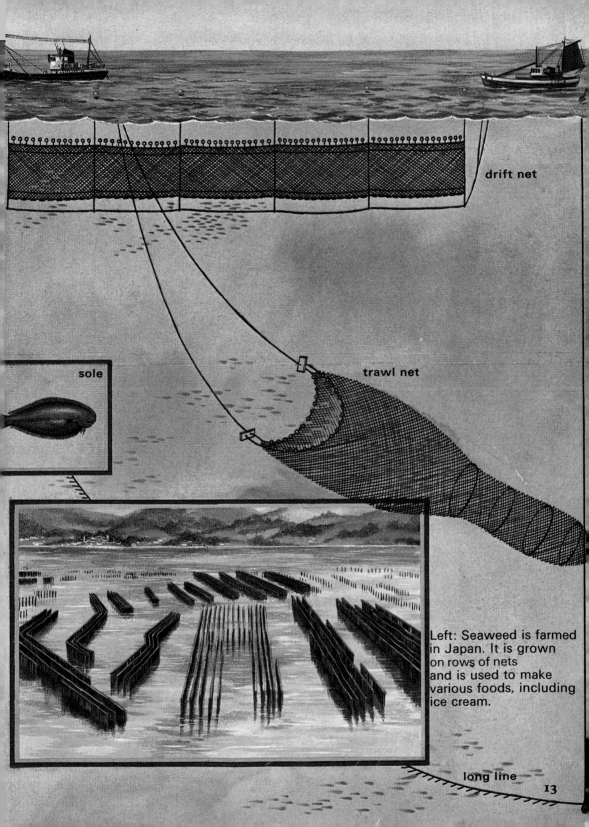

drift net

sole

trawl net

Left: Seaweed is farmed in Japan. It is grown on rows of nets and is used to make various foods, including ice cream.

long line

13

animal
plankton

chemicals
rise from
sea-bed

herring

shark

skate

The Living Ocean

The ocean is a living world, full
of plants and animals. Just as
the links of chains are fastened
together, all these living things
are linked in "food chains".

Life in the sea depends on the
Sun. The Sun's rays enable
plants such as seaweeds to make
their food. Most seaweeds are
close to the surface and many
grow near the shore.

The surface of the sea is rich
in floating life called plankton
which is made up of millions of
tiny plants and animals. The
plant plankton uses the sunlight to make food. The plankton animals feed on the plant
plankton. The animals are
mostly the microscopic young
of jellyfish, crabs and krill (a
kind of shrimp).

M. CAMM

plant
plankton

sun's rays

baleen
whale

Plankton is the main food of many fishes. Even the huge baleen whales and basking sharks eat only plankton.

Large fish, such as sharks and tuna, hunt and eat smaller fish. In shallow water there is always plenty of food for the rays, flatfish, crabs and other creatures that live on the sea-bed. In deeper waters food is scarcer. Deep-sea fish feed on each other and on the remains of dead creatures which drift down through the water.

When an animal dies, its body rots and the goodness is kept in the sea in the form of chemicals. These chemicals are carried upwards to the seaweeds and drifting plankton that use them as food. In this way the food chain keeps circling.

flounder

crab

Machines under the Sea

The first brave men to venture underwater for any length of time breathed air pumped down to them through hoses fastened to their helmets. They wore heavy boots to help keep their feet firmly on the sea-bed. Today, divers normally wear aqualungs. They carry an air supply in tanks on their backs and swim with the help of flippers. To keep warm, a diver wears a rubber "wet suit". The suit lets in enough water to form a second "skin" which is kept warm by heat from the diver's body.

Among other tasks, divers check and repair oil drilling equipment and pipelines. Welding jobs can be done inside a small airtight compartment on the sea-bed.

More and more submersible vehicles are now at work under the sea. Some have mechanical "arms". They are used for burying telephone cables and laying pipelines for oil and gas.

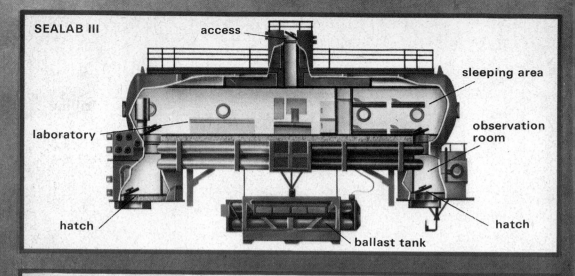

SEALAB III

access

sleeping area

observation room

laboratory

hatch

ballast tank

hatch

An Underwater Home

A diver wearing an aqualung can stay under water only as long as his air supply lasts. To explore the undersea world properly, scientists need underwater laboratories or "habitats" where they can live and work for weeks.

Sealab III is an experimental laboratory which rests on the seabed. It is rather like an undersea "space station" with its crew of divers called "aquanauts". Before entering *Sealab*, each diver must spend some time in a special chamber where his body grows accustomed to the air pressure he will experience in the vessel. To help balance the pressure of the water on the hull, the air inside *Sealab* is at a much higher pressure than the air we normally breathe.

Once they are ready for life at a depth of about 600 feet, the aquanauts are taken down to *Sealab* inside a watertight capsule. The capsule fastens on to *Sealab* and the aquanauts are soon inside their marine home. Air and electricity are piped down from a ship on the surface, and the crew keeps in touch with the world above by telephone. They can stay in *Sealab* for up to thirty days.

One day, aquanauts may live for long periods in undersea colonies, rearing fish in cages, harvesting seaweeds, and digging minerals from the ocean floor. Scientists are working on new materials, called polymers, which keep out water but let in oxygen. Future aquanauts could live inside "bubble houses", breathing through the polymer walls.

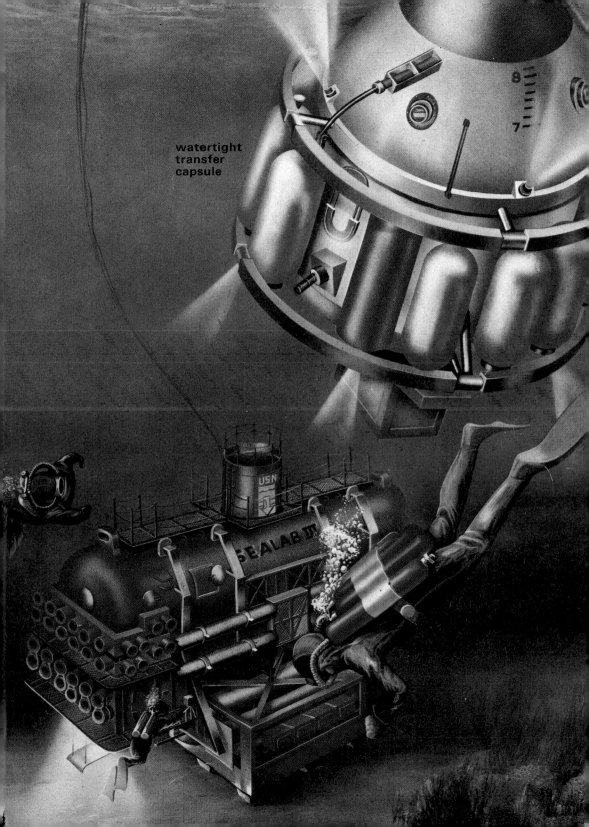

watertight
transfer
capsule

Sunken Treasure

Every underwater explorer dreams of finding sunken treasure. In the Caribbean Sea lie the wrecks of Spanish galleons together with their cargoes of gold and silver from the mines of South America.

In 1715, ten treasure ships were lost in a storm off the coast of Florida. After carefully studying old maps, divers found the wrecks and brought up the sunken gold and silver. Another famous find was the English warship *Association*, which sank off the Scilly Isles in 1702.

Divers use metal detectors to find the metal objects that lie buried in the mud and sand. As well as coins, they have found jewels, plates, cooking pots, swords and cannon. Because iron rusts in sea water, cannon must be handled with great care. Air-filled buoys lift them to the surface, where they are treated with chemicals to preserve them.

Sometimes divers have even managed to bring a complete ship to the surface. The Swedish galleon *Vasa* which sank in 1628 has been successfully raised from the sea-bed.

research
drilling
ship

Sealab III

500 ft

1000 ft

scuba diver

porcupine fish

swordfish

deep sea
diver

oarfish

Deepstar

3000 ft

deep-sea
angler fish

30,000 ft

sea-pen

Scientists believe that life on our planet began in the sea. At first the plants and animals were tiny, shapeless blobs of life. But gradually, over many, many millions of years, they evolved into all the different forms of life which are now found in the oceans and on the land.

Different plants and animals live in different parts of the sea. The richest mixture of living things is found near the surface, where the sun provides light and warmth. As the sea becomes deeper it grows colder and darker. And the variety of living things grows smaller. In the deepest parts of the oceans there is little life at all.

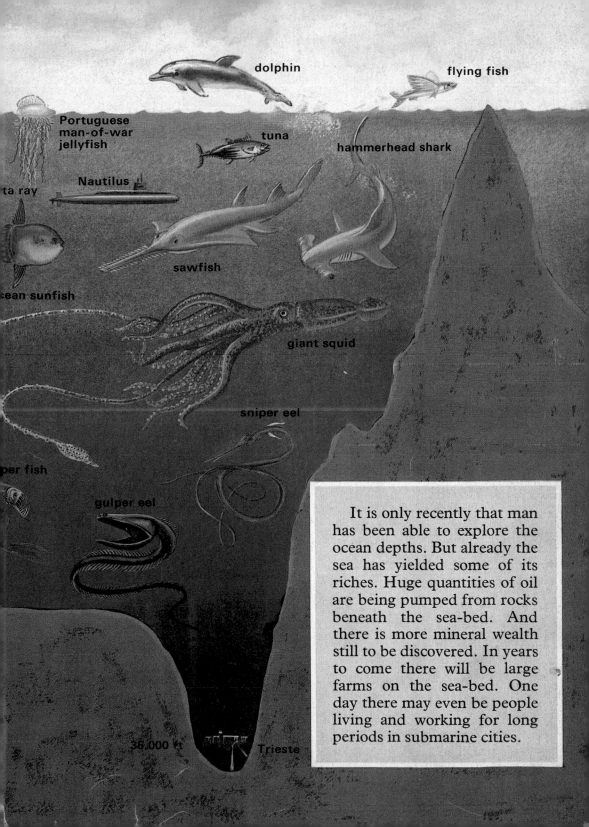

dolphin

flying fish

Portuguese
man-of-war
jellyfish

tuna

hammerhead shark

Nautilus

ta ray

sawfish

ean sunfish

giant squid

sniper eel

per fish

gulper eel

It is only recently that man has been able to explore the ocean depths. But already the sea has yielded some of its riches. Huge quantities of oil are being pumped from rocks beneath the sea-bed. And there is more mineral wealth still to be discovered. In years to come there will be large farms on the sea-bed. One day there may even be people living and working for long periods in submarine cities.

35,000 ft

Trieste